❦FLORENCE NIGHTINGALE❦

BY CHARLOTTE KOCH

ILLUSTRATED BY

MICHELE CHESSARE

DANDELION BOOKS

Published by Dandelion Press, Inc.

To Sharon and Debbie

Library of Congress Catalog Card Number 78-64424
ISBN 0-89799-038-2 pbk.   ISBN 0-89799-105-2
10 9 8 7 6 5 4 3 2 1

FLORENCE NIGHTINGALE

"Florence! Where is Florence?" called Mrs. Nightingale. She was very cross. It was time for Florence's music lesson, and she was nowhere to be found. Her older sister, Parthe, offered to look for her and soon came back dragging Florence by the skirt. Florence's face was bent down toward something fluffy she was holding in her hands.

"I'm sorry I'm late for my lesson," she mumbled without looking up.

"What are you carrying?" asked Mrs. Nightingale. Florence said nothing, but Parthe spoke up: "It's a sick bird, Mother. Flo found it outside on the ground."

"A sick bird?" shrieked Mrs. Nightingale. "Get that thing out of here! I think I shall faint!" And as Florence ran off, still holding the little bird in her hands, her mother sighed and said: "Another sick pet! I don't know what's to become of Florence!"

It was the year 1830 in England. Florence was ten and Parthe eleven. They lived together with their parents in a big house with

a beautiful garden. The Nightingales were very rich. They had cooks, maids, and gardeners to do all the chores. Mr. Nightingale did not even need to work. He was very learned and spent some of his time teaching his two daughters. His wife loved to wear pretty clothes, gossip, and go to parties, as did most of the other ladies she knew.

Mrs. Nightingale expected Parthe and Florence to become just like her when they grew up. For in those days, while boys might go to boarding school and college to prepare for a career, girls who weren't poor never lived away from home or went to work. They were kept at home and had lessons in languages, needlework, drawing, music, and dancing. They were only supposed to be pretty and ladylike and, as soon as they were old enough, to get married and live happily ever after.

All this seemed fine to Parthe. She was already a little "lady" and her mother was very pleased with her. But not with Florence! Even though Florence was pretty, she hated acting ladylike. She often fought with Parthe, a *very* unladylike thing to do. And gossip and parties bored her. She took to daydreaming, alone or even in the company of others. She was happiest nursing a sick puppy or cat or bird.

"Oh, how I wish Flo would become more like Parthe," Mrs. Nightingale complained each time Florence had done something unladylike.

"Don't worry, dear," Mr. Nightingale would answer. "Our Florence is very smart; she'll change her ways. Just give her a few more years, and she'll grow into as fine a young lady as you could wish."

As it turned out, Mr. Nightingale was both right and wrong.

Florence Nightingale did grow into a lovely young lady her mother could be proud of. She wore beautiful dresses, went to many parties, danced with handsome young men—and some of them fell in love with her. But deep down she was unchanged and nothing like her sister, her mother, and their friends. Someday, she was certain, she would do more important things than go to teas and balls.

In the summer of 1843 Florence was a young woman of twenty-three, and again Mrs. Nightingale was very upset. "Where is Florence?" she asked Parthe. "Why is it that she's never around when I want her?"

"Flo?" answered Parthe. "She's gone to the village to take a basket of food and some blankets to the Hobbses' cottage. Mr. Hobbs is out looking for work, Mrs. Hobbs is sick in bed, and there is no one to look after her four little ones." Parthe snickered. "Flo's always at the village, helping the poor."

"Florence must be out of her mind," Mrs. Nightingale replied as she shuddered. "How can she spend all her time among those people? She'll catch some horrible disease!"

But in truth Florence was never healthier or happier than when she was "among those people." There she forgot all about her daydreaming, her fights with Parthe, and her mother's scoldings, since she was doing what she liked best. Something bothered her, though: At times the good food, warm blankets, and clothes she brought were not enough to make sick people well; she needed to know more about nursing. But where was she to learn?

The problem was serious, for in Florence Nightingale's day there were no nursing schools. People believed that any woman who was kind and good would know in her heart how to care for the sick and, therefore, needed no training. Yet the women who nursed in hospitals were not even kind or good. They worked there only because they could not find a better job. No woman really wanted to work in hospitals since they were crowded, dirty,

and smelly. Sick people tried to get well at home and only entered a hospital if they were very poor and had nobody to look after them.

So when Florence asked her parents for permission to go to a nearby hospital to learn more about nursing, they made a terrible fuss.

"Florence, you must forget this dreadful idea at once," said Mrs. Nightingale and burst into tears.

"Flo, you can't mean it!" shrieked Parthe. "What will people say?"

As for Mr. Nightingale, he was so shocked he did not say anything at all.

Poor Florence! How she longed to go to work in a hospital so she could learn about nursing! But she was torn because she loved her parents and her sister and did not want them to be angry at her. So for five long years there were two Florences. The real Florence secretly got up early in the morning to study about hospitals. Then at breakfast time she turned into the other Florence, the rich young lady who tried to please her family. It was terribly hard being two people at once, and sometimes Florence thought she would go mad.

Finally in 1851, when she was thirty-one, Florence began to see that she must take matters into her own hands. She had heard that there was now a hospital in Germany where young women could learn about nursing. And even though the other three Nightingales tried to stop her, Florence decided to go there.

Her training days in Germany were long and hard, but Florence was more contented than she had ever been in her life. She was absolutely sure now that she wanted to work as a nurse. By the time she returned home, she was glad to find that her father had come over to her side. But Mrs. Nightingale and Parthe barely spoke to her. After all, had she not disgraced the family by being unladylike and stubborn and learning about nursing?

Worse was to come! Mrs. Nightingale and Parthe could hardly believe their ears when they heard what horrid thing Florence was planning next: She was going to get a job! Again they made a terrible fuss, but by now Florence wouldn't even listen. She announced that she was going to be the director of a hospital for poor ladies in London, and she would be living there.

At last, at thirty-three, she was on her own, far from Mrs. Nightingale's nagging and Parthe's complaining. Best of all, she had the work she loved to do. And she did it! Florence soon showed that she could run a hospital better than anyone else. The

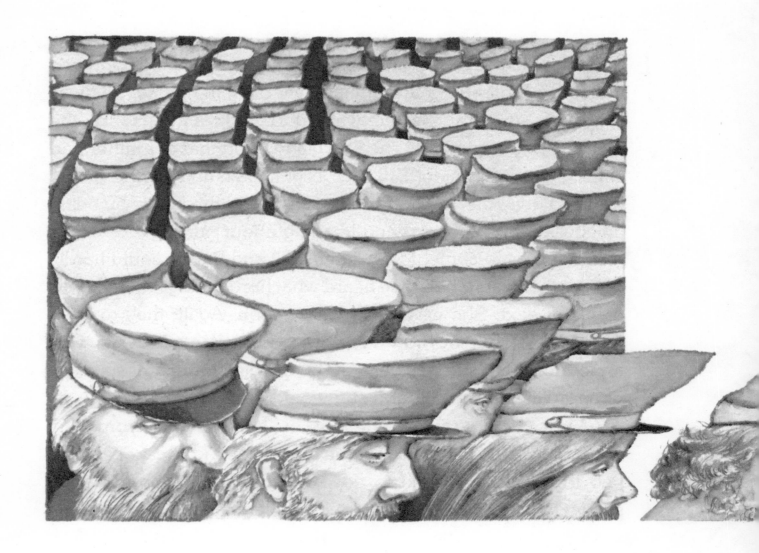

poor, sick ladies had never been so well taken care of before, and they all loved Florence for the changes she had made.

In 1854, when Florence had been running the hospital for a year, her country, England, went to war with Russia. English soldiers marched through the streets of London on their way to the ships that would take them to the faraway Crimea in Russia. People lined the sidewalks to cheer mightily, sure that their soldiers were the best and would defeat the enemy.

And they were right: Soon the newspapers told that English soldiers had fought bravely and won a great battle. But the Britons' pride quickly turned to shock when they read on: The many sick and wounded soldiers were not being given the care they needed. There were doctors but no nurses to care for the patients, just orderlies—soldiers who knew little about nursing.

The people of England were terribly angry to learn that their brave soldiers had been let down so shamefully. A committee was set up to collect money. They gathered a large sum, but money wasn't enough; what the soldiers really needed was someone who knew how to run a hospital and how to nurse the sick and wounded.

There was only one such person in England—Florence Nightingale! And so the government of England asked Florence to find forty nurses to sail with her to Scutari, where the British army had set up a hospital in a big, empty building. Florence was eager to take on the job. She wanted to show the world—and her family—what women nurses could do.

After a long tiring journey Florence and her nurses arrived at the army hospital in November of 1854. They had expected trouble, but they were shocked to discover that so much had gone wrong. The hospital was unbelievably filthy and there was a shortage of everything—beds, blankets, sheets, bandages, cooking pots, plates, even water! The food was so awful that it made the sick soldiers worse.

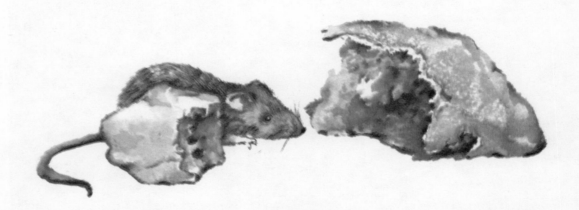

Florence wondered what had happened to all the things that had been sent to the hospital from England. She learned that some had been lost on the way, and some had arrived but had never been unloaded from the ships.

In addition, the army doctors, even though they were terribly overworked, didn't want Florence and her nurses around. Women in an army hospital! Surely they would just be in the way and make matters worse.

But when more and more sick and wounded soldiers came pouring into the hospital, the doctors were forced to change their minds and ask for Miss Nightingale's help. And Florence went into action! She had brought the money collected by the English people as well as some of her own, and she was determined to spend it well. One of the first things she bought was a supply of scrubbing brushes to clean up the hospital. She also bought operating tables, bedding and clothes for the soldiers, towels,

soap, plates, cups, knives, forks, and spoons. She started a laundry. She bought stoves and pots and food, and she and the nurses cooked special meals that the soldiers could eat. All the nurses went to work nursing the soldiers, but none worked harder than Florence. Whenever a new group of wounded soldiers was brought in, she stayed on her feet all day and all night, bandaging their wounds, making them more comfortable, and talking to them.

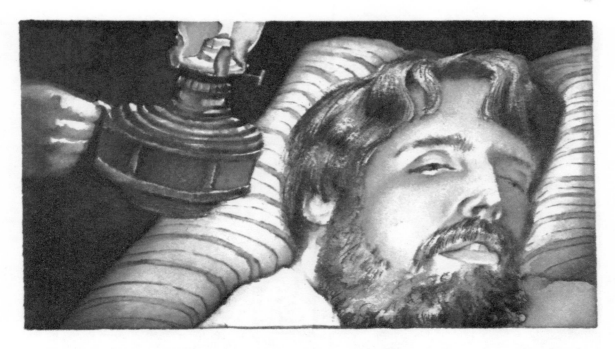

At night, when the hospital wards were nearly dark, Florence walked from bed to bed carrying a lantern. And so it was that she became known as "the Lady with a Lamp." The soldiers adored Florence. Within a few months she had managed to turn a barren, messy building into a hospital that worked. She had also shown that women could be good nurses.

So many soldiers sent home letters praising Florence that she became a famous person in England. Even Mrs. Nightingale and Parthe were impressed now and proud to be the mother and sister of Florence Nightingale, the great nurse.

Still, when the war was over and Florence came home tired and worn out from all the hard work she had done, Mrs. Nightingale and Parthe hoped that at last she would want to live like a "lady." But she didn't. Florence felt that her real work had just begun. She knew that good nurses needed training, and she meant to see that they got it. In 1860 the first real nursing school opened its doors in London with fifteen girl students who wanted to be just like the great Florence Nightingale.

Now, over a hundred years later, any girl who wants to become a nurse has many nursing schools to choose from. And she can find work in a hospital, a doctor's office, a school, or a factory. She can be nurse for her city or county, for the army, navy, or air force. What is more, boys can become nurses, too. What would Florence Nightingale think of that?